A Child's Garden of Verses

Poems by **ROBERT LOUIS STEVENSON**

Illustrated by **BRIAN WILDSMITH**

STAR BRIGHT BOOKS
NEW YORK

Published in the United States of America by Star Bright Books, Inc., New York.
The name Star Bright Books and the Star Bright Books logo are registered trademarks of Star Bright Books, Inc. Please visit www.starbrightbooks.com.

HARDCOVER ISBN-13: 978-1-59572-057-3
Previously published under ISBN:0613994647

Star Bright Books / NY / 00203100

Printed in China (WKT) 9 8 7 6 5 4 3 2

Library of Congress Cataloging-in-Publication Data

Stevenson, Robert Louis.
  A child's garden of verses / by Robert Louis Stevenson ; illustrated by Brian Wildsmith.
    p. cm.
  ISBN 978-1-59572-057-3
  1. Children's poetry, English. I. Wildsmith, Brian, ill. II. Title.

PR5489.C52 2007
821'.8--dc22
                            2007010085

To Alison Cunningham From Her Boy

For the long nights you lay awake
And watched for my unworthy sake:
For your most comfortable hand
That led me through the uneven land:
For all the story-books you read:
For all the pains you comforted:
For all you pitied, all you bore,
In sad and happy days of yore:—
My second mother, my first Wife,
The angel of my infant life—
From the sick child, now well and old,
Take, nurse, the little book you hold!

And grant it, Heaven, that all who read
May find as dear a nurse at need,
And every child who lists my rhyme,
In the bright, fireside, nursery clime,
May hear it in as kind a voice
As made my childish days rejoice!

R.L.S.

Table of Contents

Summer Sun

Great is the sun, and wide he goes
Through empty heaven without repose;
And in the blue and glowing days
More thick than rain he showers his rays.

Though closer still the blinds we pull
To keep the shady parlor cool,
Yet he will find a chink or two
To slip his golden fingers through.

The dusty attic spider-clad
He, through the keyhole, maketh glad;
And through the broken edge of tiles,
Into the laddered hayloft smiles.

Meantime his golden face around
He bares to all the garden ground,
And sheds a warm and glittering look
Among the ivy's inmost nook.

Above the hills, along the blue,
Round the bright air with footing true
To please the child, to paint the rose,
The gardener of the World, he goes.

Looking-Glass River

Smooth it slides upon its travel,
 Here a wimple, there a gleam—
  O the clean gravel!
  O the smooth stream!

  Sailing blossoms, silver fishes,
   Paven pools as clear as air—
  How a child wishes
  To live down there!

We can see our colored faces
 Floating on the shaken pool
  Down in cool places,
  Dim and very cool;

   Till a wind or water wrinkle,
    Dipping marten, plumping trout,
     Spreads in a twinkle
     And blots all out.

    See the rings pursue each other;
     All below grows black as night,
     Just as if mother
     Had blown out the light!

    Patience, children, just a minute
     See the spreading circles die;
      The stream and all in it
        Will clear by-and-by.

The Cow

The friendly cow all red and white,
I love with all my heart:
She gives me cream with all her might,
To eat with apple-tart.

She wanders lowing here and there,
And yet she cannot stray,
All in the pleasant open air,
The pleasant light of day;

And blown by all the winds that pass
And wet with all the showers,
She walks among the meadow grass
And eats the meadow flowers.

Bed in Summer

In winter I get up at night
And dress by yellow candle-light.
In summer, quite the other way,
I have to go to bed by day.

I have to go to bed and see
The birds still hopping on the tree,
Or hear the grown-up people's feet
Still going past me on the street.

And does it not seem hard to you,
When all the sky is clear and blue,
And I should like so much to play,
To have to go to bed by day?

The Moon

The moon has a face like the clock in the hall;
She shines on thieves on the garden wall,
On streets and fields and harbor quays,
And birdies asleep in the forks of the trees.

The squalling cat and the squeaking mouse,
The howling dog by the door of the house,
The bat that lies in bed at noon,
All love to be out by the light of the moon.

But all of the things that belong to the day
Cuddle to sleep to be out of her way;
And flowers and children close their eyes
Till up in the morning the sun shall arise.

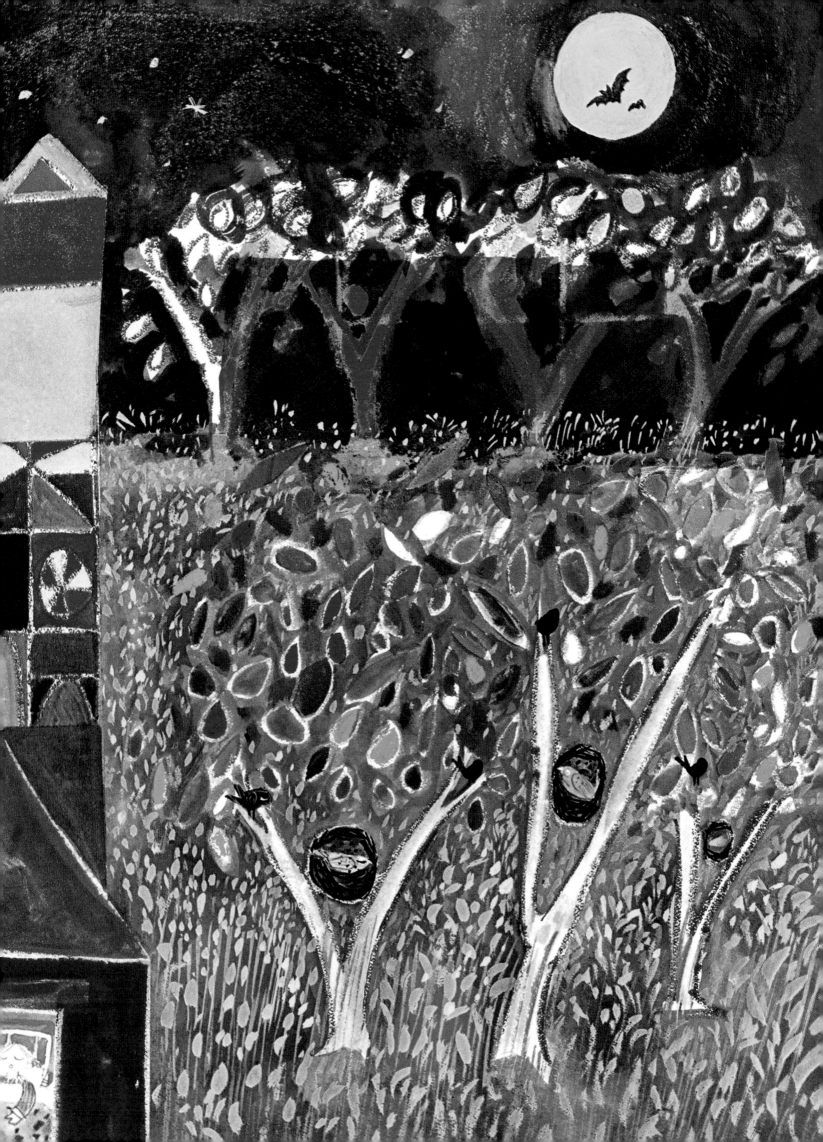

Where Go the Boats?

Dark brown is the river,
   Golden is the sand.
It flows along forever,
   With trees on either hand.

Green leaves a-floating,
   Castles of the foam,
Boats of mine-a-boating—
   Where will all come home?

On goes the river
   And out past the mill,
Away down the valley,
   Away down the hill.

Away down the river,
   A hundred miles or more,
Other little children
   Shall bring my boats ashore.

The Swing

How do you like to go up in a swing,
   Up in the air so blue?
Oh, I do think it the pleasantest thing
   Ever a child can do!

Up in the air and over the wall,
   Till I can see so wide,
Rivers and trees and cattle and all
   Over the countryside—

Till I look down on the garden green,
   Down on the roof so brown—
Up in the air I go flying again,
   Up in the air and down.

Happy Thought

The world is full of a number of things,
   I'm sure we should all be as happy as kings.

My Shadow

I have a little shadow that goes in and out with me,
  And what can be the use of him is more than I can see.
He is very, very like me from the heels up to the head;
  And I see him jump before me, when I jump into my bed.

The funniest thing about him is the way he likes to grow—
  Not at all like proper children, which is always very slow;
For he sometimes shoots up taller like an india-rubber ball,
  And he sometimes gets so little that there's none of him at all.

He hasn't got a notion of how children ought to play,
  And can only make a fool of me in every sort of way.
He stays so close beside me, he's a coward you can see;
  I'd think shame to stick to nursie as that shadow sticks to me!

One morning, very early, before the sun was up,
  I rose and found the shining dew on every buttercup;
But my lazy little shadow, like an arrant sleepy-head,
  Had stayed at home behind me and was fast asleep in bed.

Auntie's Skirts

Whenever Auntie moves around,
  Her dresses make a curious sound,
    They trail behind her up the floor,
      And trundle after through the door.

The Dumb Soldier

When the grass was closely mown,
Walking on the lawn alone,
In the turf a hole I found,
And hid a soldier underground.

Spring and daisies came apace;
Grasses hide my hiding place;
Grasses run like a green sea
O'er the lawn up to my knee.

Under grass alone he lies,
Looking up with leaden eyes,
Scarlet coat and pointed gun,
To the stars and to the sun.

When the grass is ripe like grain,
When the scythe is stoned again,
When the lawn is shaven clear,
Then my hole shall reappear.

I shall find him, never fear,
I shall find my grenadier;
But for all that's gone and come,
I shall find my soldier dumb.

He has lived, a little thing,
In the grassy woods of spring;
Done, if he could tell me true,
Just as I should like to do.

He has seen the starry hours
And the springing of the flowers;
And the fairy things that pass
In the forests of the grass.

In the silence he has heard
Talking bee and ladybird,
And the butterfly has flown
O'er him as he lay alone.

Not a word will he disclose,
Not a word of all he knows.
I must lay him on the shelf,
And make up the tale myself.

My Ship and I

O it's I that am the captain of a tidy little ship,
   Of a ship that goes a-sailing on the pond;
And my ship it keeps a-turning all around and all about;
But when I'm a little older, I shall find the secret out
   How to send my vessel sailing on beyond.

For I mean to grow as little as the dolly at the helm,
   And the dolly I intend to come alive;
And with him beside to help me, it's a sailing I shall go,
It's a–sailing on the water, when the jolly breezes blow
   And the vessel goes a divie-divie-dive.

      O it's then you'll see me sailing through the rushes and the reeds,
         And you'll hear the water singing at the prow;
      For beside the dolly sailor, I'm to voyage and explore,
      To land upon the island where no dolly was before,
         and to fire the penny cannon in the bow.

Nest Eggs

Birds all the sunny day
　　Flutter and quarrel
Here in the arbor-like
　　Tent of the laurel.

Here in the fork
　　The brown nest is seated;
Four little blue eggs
　　The mother keeps heated.

While we stand watching her
　　Staring like gabies,
Safe in each egg are the
　　Bird's little babies.

Soon the frail eggs they shall
　　Chip, and upspringing
Make all the April woods
　　Merry with singing.

Younger than we are,
　　O children, and frailer,
Soon in blue air they'll be,
　　Singer and sailor.

We, so much older,
　　Taller and stronger,
We shall look down on the
　　Birdies no longer.

They shall go flying
　　With musical speeches
High overhead in the
　　Tops of the beeches.

In spite of our wisdom
　　And sensible talking,
We on our feet must go
　　Plodding and walking.

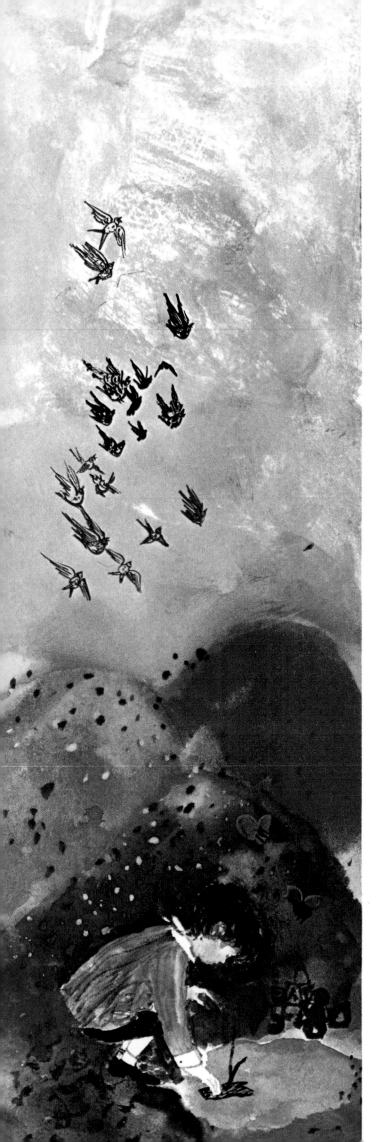

My Kingdom

Down by a shining water well
I found a very little dell,
  No higher than my head.
The heather and the gorse about
In summer bloom were coming out,
  Some yellow and some red.

I called the little pool a sea;
The little hills were big to me;
  For I am very small.
I made a boat, I made a town,
I searched the caverns up and down,
  And named them one and all.

And all about was mine, I said,
The little sparrows overhead,
  The little minnows too.
This was the world and I was king;
For me the bees came by to sing,
For me the swallows flew.

I played there were no deeper seas,
Nor any wider plains than these,
  Nor other kings than me.
At last I heard my mother call
Out from the house at evenfall,
  To call me home to tea.

And I must rise and leave my dell,
And leave my dimpled water well,
  And leave my heather blooms.
Alas! and as my home I neared,
How very big my nurse appeared.
  How great and cool the rooms!

My Bed Is a Boat

My bed is like a little boat;
Nurse helps me in when I embark;
She girds me in my sailor's coat
And starts me in the dark.

At night, I go on board and say
Good-night to all my friends on shore;
I shut my eyes and sail away
And see and hear no more.

And sometimes things to bed I take,
As prudent sailors have to do;
Perhaps a slice of wedding-cake,
Perhaps a toy or two.

All night across the dark we steer;
But when the day returns at last,
Safe in my room, beside the pier,
I find my vessel fast.

Historical Associations

Dear Uncle Jim, this garden ground
That now you smoke your pipe around,
Has seen immortal actions done
And valiant battles lost and won.

Here we had best on tip-toe tread,
While I for safety march ahead,
For this is that enchanted ground
Where all who loiter slumber sound.

Here is the sea, here is the sand,
Here is the simple Shepherd's Land,
Here are the fairy hollyhocks,
And there are Ali Baba's rocks.

But yonder, see! apart and high,
Frozen Siberia lies; where I,
With Robert Bruce and William Tell,
Was bound by an enchanter's spell.

There, then, awhile in chains we lay,
In wintry dungeons, far from day;
But ris'n at length, with might and main,
Our iron fetters burst in twain.

Then all the horns were blown in town;
And to the ramparts clanging down,
All the giants leaped to horse
And charged behind us through the gorse.

On we rode, the others and I,
Over the mountains blue, and by
The Silver River, the sounding sea
And the robber woods of Tartary.

A thousand miles we galloped fast,
And down the witches' lane we passed,
And rode amain, with brandished sword,
Up to the middle, through the ford.

Last we drew rein—a weary three—
Upon the lawn, in time for tea,
And from our steeds alighted down
Before the gates of Babylon.

The Hayloft

Through all the pleasant meadow-side
The grass grew shoulder-high,
Till the shining scythes went far and wide
And cut it down to dry.

These green and sweetly smelling crops
They led in wagons home;
And they piled them here in mountain tops
For mountaineers to roam.

Here is Mount Clear, Mount Rusty-Nail,
Mount Eagle and Mount High;—
The mice that in these mountains dwell,
No happier than I!

Oh, what a joy to clamber there,
Oh, what a place for play,
With the sweet, the dim, the dusty air,
The happy hills of hay!

Keepsake Mill

Over the borders, a sin without pardon,
　Breaking the branches and crawling below,
Out through the breach in the wall of the garden,
　Down by the banks of the river, we go.

Here is the mill with the humming of thunder,
　Here is the weir with the wonder of foam,
Here is the sluice with the race running under—
　Marvellous places, though handy to home!

Sounds of the village grow stiller and stiller,
　Stiller the note of the birds on the hill;
Dusty and dim are the eyes of the miller,
　Deaf are his ears with the moil of the mill.

Years may go by, and the wheel in the river
　Wheel as it wheels for us, children, today,
Wheel and keep roaring the foaming for ever
　Long after all of the boys are away.

Home from the Indies and home from the ocean,
　Heroes and soldiers we all shall come home;
Still we shall find the old mill wheel in motion,
　Turning and churning that river to foam.

You with the bean that I gave when we quarreled,
　I with your marble of Saturday last,
Honoured and old and all gaily apparelled,
　Here we shall meet and remember the past.

Farewell to the Farm

The coach is at the door at last;
The eager children, mounting fast
And kissing hands, in chorus sing:
Good-bye, good-bye, to everything!

To house and garden, field and lawn,
The meadow-gates we swang upon,
To pump and stable, tree and swing,
Good-bye, good-bye, to everything!

And fare you well for evermore,
O ladder at the hayloft door,
O hayloft where the cobwebs cling,
Good-bye, good-bye, to everything!

Crack goes the whip, and off we go;
The trees and the houses smaller grow;
Last, round the woody turn we swing:
Good-bye, good-bye, to everything!

Travel

I should like to rise and go
Where the golden apples grow;—
Where below another sky
Parrot islands anchored lie,
And, watched by cockatoos and goats,
Lonely Crusoes building boats;—
Where in sunshine reaching out
Eastern cities, miles about,
Are with mosque and minaret
Among sandy gardens set,
And the rich goods from near and far
Hang for sale in the bazaar;—
Where the Great Wall round China goes,
And on one side the desert blows,
And with bell and voice and drum,
Cities on the other hum;—
Where are forests, hot as fire,
Wide as England, tall as a spire,
Full of apes and cocoa-nuts
And the brave hunters' huts;—
Where the knotty crocodile
Lies and blinks in the Nile,
And the red flamingo flies
Hunting fish before his eyes;—
Where in jungles, near and far,
Man-devouring tigers are,
Lying close and giving ear
Lest the hunt be drawing near,
Or a comer-by be seen
Swinging in a palanquin;—
Where among the desert sands
Some deserted city stands,
All its children, sweep and prince,
Grown to manhood ages since,
Not a foot in street or house,
Not a stir of child or mouse,
And when kindly falls the night,
In all the town no spark of light.

There I'll come when I'm a man
With a camel caravan;
Light a fire in the gloom
Of some dusty dining-room;
See the pictures on the walls,
Heroes, fights and festivals;
And in a corner find the toys
Of the old Egyptian boys.

My Treasures

These nuts, that I keep in the back of the nest
Where all my lead soldiers are lying at rest,
Were gathered in autumn by nursie and me
In a wood with a well by the side of the sea.

This whistle we made (and how clearly it sounds!)
By the side of a field at the end of the grounds.
Of a branch of a plane, with a knife of my own,
It was nursie who made it, and nursie alone!

The stone, with the white and the yellow and grey,
We discovered I cannot tell *how* far away;
And I carried it back although weary and cold,
For though father denies it, I'm sure it is gold.

But of all my treasures the last is the king,
For there's very few children possess such a thing;
And that is a chisel, both handle and blade,
Which a man who was really a carpenter made.

Time to Rise

A birdie with a yellow bill
Hopped upon the window sill,
Cocked his shining eye and said:
"Ain't you 'shamed, you sleepy-head?"

The Little Land

When at home alone I sit,
And am very tired of it,
I have just to shut my eyes
To go sailing through the skies—
    To go sailing far away
To the pleasant Land of Play;
    To the fairy land afar
Where the Little People are;
Where the clover-tops are trees,
And the rain-pools are the seas,
And the leaves, like little ships,
    Sail about on tiny trips;
    And above the daisy tree
        Through the grasses,
High o'erhead the Bumble Bee
        Hums and passes.

    In that forest to and fro
    I can wander, I can go;
See the spider and the fly,
And the ants go marching by,
Carrying parcels with their feet
Down the green and grassy street.
    I can in the sorrel sit
Where the ladybird alit.
I can climb the jointed grass
    And on high
See the greater swallows pass
    In the sky,
And the round sun rolling by
Heeding no such things as I.

Through that forest I can pass
Till, as in a looking-glass,
Humming fly and daisy tree
And my tiny self I see,
Painted very clear and neat
On the rain-pool at my feet.
Should a leaflet come to land
Drifting near to where I stand,
Straight I'll board that tiny boat
Round the rain-pool sea to float.

Little thoughtful creatures sit
On the grassy coasts of it;
Little things with lovely eyes
See me sailing with surprise.
Some are clad in armour green—
(These have sure to battle been!)—
Some are pied with ev'ry hue,
Black and crimson, gold and blue;
Some have wings and swift are gone;—
But they all look kindly on.

When my eyes I once again
Open, and see all things plain:
High bare walls, great bare floor;
Great big knobs on drawer and door;
Great big people perched on chairs,
Stitching tucks and mending tears,
Each a hill that I could climb,
And talking nonsense all the time—
    O dear me,
    That I could be
  A sailor on the rain-pool sea,
  A climber in the clover tree,
    And just come back, a sleepy-head,
    Late at night to go to bed.

The Flowers

All the names I know from nurse:
Gardener's garters, Shepherd's purse,
Bachelor's buttons, Lady's smock,
and the Lady Hollyhock.

Fairy places, fairy things,
Fairy woods where the wild bee wings,
Tiny trees for tiny dames—
These must all be fairy names!

Tiny woods below whose boughs
Shady fairies weave a house;
Tiny tree-tops, rose or thyme,
Where the braver fairies climb!

Fair are grown-up people's trees,
But the fairest woods are these;
Where, if I were not so tall,
I should live for good and all.

Foreign Lands

Up into the cherry tree
Who should climb but little me?
   I held the trunk with both my hands
   And looked abroad on foreign lands.

I saw the next door garden lie,
Adorned with flowers, before my eye,
   And many pleasant places more
   That I had never seen before.

I saw the dimpling river pass
And be the sky's blue looking-glass;
   The dusty roads go up and down
   With people tramping in to town.

If I could find a higher tree
Farther and farther I should see,
   To where the grown-up river slips
   Into the sea among the ships,

To where the roads on either hand
Lead onward into fairy land,
   Where all the children dine at five,
   And all the playthings come alive.

Block City

What are you able to build with your blocks?
Castles and palaces, temples and docks.
Rain may keep raining, and others go roam,
But I can be happy and building at home.

Let the sofa be mountains, the carpet be sea,
There I'll establish a city for me:
A kirk and a mill and a palace beside,
And a harbour as well where my vessels may ride.

Great is the palace with pillar and wall,
A sort of a tower on the top of it all,
And steps coming down in an orderly way
To where my toy vessels lie safe in the bay.

This one is sailing and that one is moored:
Hark to the song of the sailors on board!
And see, on the steps of my palace, the kings
Coming and going with presents and things!

Now I have down with it, down let it go!
All in a moment the town is laid low.
Block upon block lying scattered and free,
What is there left of my town by the sea?

Yet as I saw it, I see it again,
The kirk and the palace, the ships and the men,
And as long as I live and where'er I may be,
I'll always remember my town by the sea.

The Wind

I saw you toss the kites on high
And blow the birds about the sky;
And all around I heard you pass,
Like ladies' skirts across the grass—
    O wind, a-blowing all day long,
    O wind, that sings so loud a song!

I saw the different things you did,
But always you yourself you hid.
I felt you push, I heard you call,
I could not see yourself at all—
    O wind, a-blowing all day long,
    O wind, that sings so loud a song!

O you that are so strong and cold,
O blower, are you young or old?
Are you a beast of field and tree,
Or just a stronger child than me?
    O wind, a-blowing all day long,
    O wind, that sings so loud a song!

Young Night-Thought

All night long and every night,
When my mamma puts out the light,
I see the people marching by,
As plain as day, before my eye.

Armies and emperors and kings,
All carrying different kinds of things,
And marching in so grand a way,
You never saw the like by day.

So fine a show was never seen
At the great circus on the green;
For every kind of beast and man
Is marching in that caravan.

At first they move a little slow,
But still the faster on they go,
And still beside them close I keep
Until we reach the town of Sleep.

Windy Nights

Whenever the moon and stars are set,
Whenever the wind is high,
All night long in the dark and wet,
A man goes riding by.
Late in the night when the fires are out,
Why does he gallop and gallop about?

Whenever the trees are crying aloud,
And ships are tossed at sea,
By, on the highway, low and loud,
By at the gallop goes he.
By at the gallop he goes, and then
By he comes back at the gallop again.

Picture Books in Winter

Summer fading, winter comes—
Frosty mornings, tingling thumbs,
Window robins, wintry rooks,
And the picture story-books.

Water now is turned to stone
Nurse and I can walk upon;
Still we find the flowing brooks
In the picture story-books.

All the pretty things put by,
Wait upon the children's eye,
Sheep and shepherds, trees and crooks,
In the picture story-books.

We may see how all things are,
Seas and cities, near and far,
And the flying fairies' looks,
In the picture story-books.

How am I to sing your praise,
Happy chimney-corner days,
Sitting safe in nursery nooks,
Reading picture story-books.

The Land of Nod

From breakfast on through all the day
At home among my friends I stay,
But every night I go abroad
Afar into the land of Nod.

All by myself I have to go,
With none to tell me what to do—
All alone beside the streams
And up the mountain-sides of dreams.

The strangest things are there for me,
Both things to eat and things to see,
And many frightening sights abroad
Till morning in the land of Nod.

Try as I like to find the way,
I never can get back by day,
Nor can remember plain and clear
The curious music that I hear.

The Land of Counterpane

When I was sick and lay a-bed,
I had two pillows at my head,
And all my toys beside me lay
To keep me happy all the day.

And sometimes for an hour or so
I watched my leaden soldiers go,
With different uniforms and drills,
Among the bed-clothes, through the hills;

And sometimes sent my ships in fleets
All up and down among the sheets;
Or brought my trees and houses out,
And planted cities all about.

I was the giant great and still
That sits upon the pillow-hill,
And sees before him, dale and plain,
The pleasant land of counterpane.

From a Railway Carriage

Faster than fairies, faster than witches,
Bridges and houses, hedges and ditches;
And charging along like troops in a battle
All through the meadows the horses and cattle:
All of the sights of the hill and the plain
Fly as thick as driving rain;
And ever again, in the wink of an eye,
Painted stations whistle by.

Here is a child who clambers and scrambles,
All by himself and gathering brambles;
Here is a tramp who stands and gazes;
And there is the green for stringing the daisies
Here is a cart run away in the road
Lumping along with man and load;
And here is a mill and there is a river:
Each a glimpse and gone for ever!

At the Sea-Side

When I was down beside the sea
A wooden spade they gave to me
To dig the sandy shore.
My holes were empty like a cup.
In every hole the sea came up,
Till it could come no more.

Looking Forward

When I am grown to man's estate
I shall be very proud and great,
And tell the other girls and boys
Not to meddle with my toys.

Rain

The rain is raining all around,
It falls on field and tree,
It rains on the umbrellas here,
And on the ships at sea.

Night and Day

When the golden day is done,
  Through the closing portal,
Child and garden, flower and sun,
  Vanish all things mortal.

As the blinding shadows fall
  As the rays diminish,
Under evening's cloak, they all
  Roll away and vanish.

Garden darkened, daisy shut,
  Child in bed, they slumber—
Glow-worm in the highway rut,
  Mice among the lumber.

In the darkness houses shine,
  Parents move with candles;
Till on all, the night divine
  Turns the bedroom handles.

Till at last the day begins
  In the east a-breaking,
In the hedges and the whins
  Sleeping birds a-waking.

In the darkness shapes of things,
  Houses, trees, and hedges,
Clearer grow; and sparrow's wings
  Beat on window ledges.

These shall wake the yawning maid;
    She the door shall open—
Finding dew on garden glade
    And the morning broken.

There my garden grows again
    Green and rosy painted,
As at eve behind the pane
    From my eyes it fainted.

Just as it was shut away,
    Toy-like, in the even,
Here I see it glow with day
    Under glowing heaven.

Every path and every plot,
    Every bush of roses,
Every blue forget-me-not
    Where the dew reposes.

"Up!" they cry, "the day is come
    On the smiling valleys:
We have beat the morning drum;
    Playmate, join your allies!"

Autumn Fires

In the other gardens
And all up the vale,
From the autumn bonfires
See the smoke trail!

Pleasant summer over
And all the summer flowers,
The red fire blazes,
The grey smoke towers.

Sing a song of seasons!
Something bright in all!
Flowers in the summer,
Fires in the fall!

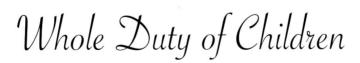

Whole Duty of Children

A child should always say what's true
And speak when he is spoken to,
And behave mannerly at table;
At least as far as he is able.

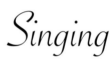

Singing

Of speckled eggs the birdie sings
   And nests among the trees;
The sailor sings of ropes and things
   In ships upon the seas.

The children sing in far Japan,
   The children sing in Spain;
The organ with the organ man
   Is singing in the rain.

The Lamplighter

My tea is nearly ready and the sun has left the sky.
It's time to take the window to see Leerie going by;
For every night at teatime and before you take your seat,
With lantern and with ladder he comes posting up the street.

Now Tom would be a driver and Maria go to sea,
And my papa's a banker and as rich as he can be;
But I, when I am stronger and can choose what I'm to do,
O Leerie, I'll go round at night and light the lamps with you!

For we are very lucky, with a lamp before the door,
And Leerie stops to light it as he lights so many more;
And oh! before you hurry by with ladder and with light;
O Leerie, see a little child and nod to him tonight!

North-West Passage

1. Good-Night

When the bright lamp is carried in,
The sunless hours again begin;
O'er all without, in field and lane,
The haunted night returns again.

Now we behold the embers flee
About the firelit hearth; and see
Our faces painted as we pass,
Like pictures, on the window-glass.

Must we to bed indeed? Well then,
Let us arise and go like men,
And face with an undaunted tread
The long black passage up to bed.

Farewell, O brother, sister, sire!
O pleasant party round the fire!
The songs you sing, the tales you tell,
Till far tomorrow, fare ye well!

2. Shadow March

All round the house is the jet-black night;
It stares through the window-pane;
It crawls in the corners, hiding from the light,
And it moves with the moving flame.

Now my little heart goes a-beating like a drum,
With the breath of the Bogie in my hair;
And all round the candle the crooked shadows come,
And go marching along up the stair.

The shadow of the balusters, the shadow of the lamp,
The shadow of the child that goes to bed—
All the wicked shadows coming, tramp, tramp, tramp,
With the black night overhead.

3. In Port

Last, to the chamber where I lie
My fearful footsteps patter nigh,
And come from out the cold and gloom
Into my warm and cheerful room.

There, safe arrived, we turn about
To keep the coming shadows out,
And close the happy door at last
On all the perils that we passed.

Then, when mamma goes by to bed
She shall come in with tip-toe tread,
And see me lying warm and fast
And in the Land of Nod at last.

Escape at Bedtime

The lights from the parlour and kitchen shone out
    Through the blinds and the windows and bars;
And high overhead and all moving about,
    There were thousands of millions of stars.
There ne'er were such thousands of leaves on a tree,
    Nor of people in church or the Park,
As the crowds of the stars that looked down upon me,
    And that glittered and winked in the dark.

The Dog, and the Plough, and the Hunter, and all,
    And the star of the sailor, and Mars,
These shone in the sky, and the pail by the wall
    Would be half full of water and stars.
They saw me at last, and they chased me with cries,
    And they soon had me packed into bed;
But the glory kept shining and bright in my eyes,
    And the stars going round in my head.

Pirate Story

Three of us afloat in the meadow by the swing,
  Three of us aboard in the basket on the lea.
Winds are in the air, they are blowing in the spring,
  And waves are on the meadow like the waves there are at sea.

Where shall we adventure, today that we're afloat,
  Wary of the weather and steering by a star?
Shall it be to Africa, a-steering off the boat,
  To Providence, or Babylon, or off to Malabar?

Hi! but here's a squadron a-rowing on the sea—
  Cattle on the meadow a-charging with a roar!
Quick, and we'll escape them, they're as mad as they can be,
  The wicket is the harbour and the garden is the shore.

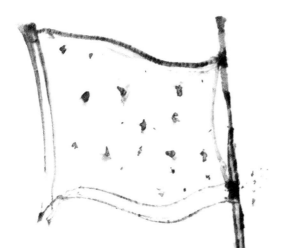

Marching Song

Bring the comb and play upon it!
Marching, here we come!
Willie cocks his highland bonnet,
Johnnie beats the drum.

Mary Jane commands the party,
Peter leads the rear;
Feet in time, alert and hearty,
Each a Grenadier!

All in the most martial manner
Marching double-quick;
While the napkin like a banner
Waves upon the stick!

Here's enough of fame and pillage,
Great Commander Jane!
Now that we've been round the village,
Let's go home again.

Winter-Time

Late lies the wintry sun a-bed,
A frosty, fiery sleepy-head;
Blinks but an hour or two; and then,
A blood-red orange, sets again.

Before the stars have left the skies,
At morning in the dark I rise;
And shivering in my nakedness,
By the cold candle, bathe and dress.

Close by the jolly fire I sit
To warm my frozen bones a bit;
Or with a reindeer-sled, explore
The colder countries round the door.

When to go out, my nurse doth wrap
Me in my comforter and cap:
The cold wind burns my face, and blows
Its frosty pepper up my nose.

Black are my steps on silver sod;
Thick blows my frosty breath abroad;
And tree and house, and hill and lake,
And frosted like a wedding-cake.

Index